EUROPEAN PAINTINGS IN THE METROPOLITAN MUSEUM OF ART

by artists born in or before 1865

A SUMMARY CATALOGUE

by Katharine Baetjer

Associate Curator, Department of European Paintings

VOLUME TWO

The Metropolitan Museum of Art
New York

Copyright © 1980 by The Metropolitan Museum of Art

LIBRARY OF CONGRESS CATALOGING IN PUBLICATION DATA

New York (City). Metropolitan Museum of Art.
 European paintings in The Metropolitan Museum of Art.

 Includes index.
 1. Painting, European—Catalogs. 2. Painting—New
York (City)—Catalogs. 3. New York (City). Metropolitan
Museum of Art—Catalogs. I. Baetjer, Katharine.
II. Title.

ND450.N45 1980 759.94′074′01471 80–17747
ISBN 0–87099–250–3

PUBLISHED BY

The Metropolitan Museum of Art, New York

Bradford D. Kelleher, Publisher
John P. O'Neill, Editor in Chief
Ellen Shultz, Editor
Peter Oldenburg, Designer

Photographs by the Photograph Studio, The Metro-
 politan Museum of Art
Composition by Graphic Composition, Inc., Athens,
 Georgia
Printed by Murray Printing Company, Westford,
 Massachusetts
Bound by American Book-Stratford Press, Inc.,
 Saddle Brook, New Jersey

CONTENTS

VOLUME ONE: Text

Preface vii

Note to the Catalogue ix

Catalogue 1

Index 201

VOLUME TWO: Illustrations

Italian Paintings

 Florentine 1

 Sienese 43

 Central and South Italian 77

 Venetian 107

 North Italian 145

 XIX century 179

Spanish Paintings (including Portuguese
and Peruvian) 183

Icons (including Byzantine, Post-Byzantine,
and Russian) 221

Russian Paintings 239

British Paintings 245

German Paintings (including Austrian,
Czechoslovakian, Danish, Hungarian,
Swedish, and Swiss) 287

VOLUME THREE: Illustrations

Flemish Paintings (including Dutch and
Portuguese) 325

Dutch Paintings, XVII and XVIII century 393

Dutch and Belgian Paintings, XIX century 459

French Paintings

 middle XV–XVII century 467

 XVIII century 493

 XIX century 535

ITALIAN PAINTINGS

FLORENTINE, XIII–XVII CENTURY

60.173 Berlinghiero

69.280.4 Florentine, last quarter XIII century

41.100.8 Master of the Magdalen

64.189.1 Master of the Magdalen

Italian/Florentine

11.126.1 Giotto

1975.1.60 Follower of Giotto

1971.115.1a Follower of Giotto

1971.115.1b Follower of Giotto

41.100.21 Florentine, late XIII century

49.39 Master of Varlungo

64.189.3a Pacino di Bonaguida

64.189.3b Pacino di Bonaguida

43.98.13 Maso di Banco

43.98.3 Bernardo Daddi

41.190.15 Bernardo Daddi

43.98.4 Bernardo Daddi

1975.1.58 Bernardo Daddi

1975.1.59 Bernardo Daddi

41.190.12 Workshop of Bernardo Daddi

32.100.70 Workshop of Bernardo Daddi

7

41.100.15 Workshop of Bernardo Daddi

1974.217 Follower of Bernardo Daddi

47.143 Florentine, 2nd quarter XIV century

63.203 Florentine, 2nd quarter XIV century

10.97 Taddeo Gaddi

07.200 Giovanni da Milano

25.120.241 Niccolò di Tommaso

1975.1.65 Followers of Andrea Orcagna

27.231a Master of the Orcagnesque Misericordia

27.231b Master of the Orcagnesque Misericordia

1975.1.69 Master of the Santa Verdiana Triptych

50.229.2 Florentine, dated 1394

12.41.4 Giovanni di Bartolommeo Cristiani

12.41.3 Giovanni di Bartolommeo Cristiani

12.41.1 Giovanni di Bartolommeo Cristiani

12.41.2 Giovanni di Bartolommeo Cristiani

41.100.33 Agnolo Gaddi

41.190.23 Workshop of Agnolo Gaddi

1975.1.62 Follower of Agnolo Gaddi

53.37 Florentine, early XV century

13.175 Spinello Aretino

13.175 Spinello Aretino

1975.1.63- 64 Spinello Aretino

88.3.77 Florentine, early XV century

65.14.1 Lorenzo Monaco

65.14.2 Lorenzo Monaco

65.14.3 Lorenzo Monaco

65.14.4 Lorenzo Monaco

1975.1.67 Lorenzo Monaco

1975.1.66 Lorenzo Monaco

09.91 Workshop of Lorenzo Monaco

30.95.254 Florentine, 2nd quarter XV century

15

43.98.5 Giovanni di Francesco Toscani

58.135 Lorenzo di Niccolò di Martino

26.287.1 Workshop of Lorenzo di Niccolò di Martino

26.287.2 Workshop of Lorenzo di Niccolò di Martino

1975.1.68 Bicci di Lorenzo

41.100.16 Bicci di Lorenzo

88.3.89 Bicci di Lorenzo

16.121 Bicci di Lorenzo

14.40.628 Fra Angelico

24.22 Workshop of Fra Angelico

41.190.8 Workshop of Fra Angelico

1971.115.4 Paolo di Stefano Badaloni

32.75.2a – c Florentine, 1st quarter XV century

18.117.2 Marco del Buono and Apollonio di Giovanni
14.39 Marco del Buono and Apollonio di Giovanni

41.190.129, 130 Florentine?, 2nd quarter XV century

32.75.1a – c Marco del Buono and Apollonio di Giovanni

49.7.9 Fra Filippo Lippi

89.15.19 Fra Filippo Lippi

17.89 Fra Filippo Lippi

1975.1.70ab Fra Filippo Lippi

43.98.2 Fra Filippo Lippi

35.31.1a Fra Filippo Lippi

35.31.1c Fra Filippo Lippi

35.31.1b Fra Filippo Lippi

29.100.17 Follower of Fra Filippo Lippi

19.87 Domenico di Michelino

1975.1.71 Neri di Bicci

1975.1.72 Neri di Bicci

50.145.30 Pesellino

65.181.4 Lippi-Pesellino Imitators

32.100.79 Lippi-Pesellino Imitators

41.100.9 Lippi-Pesellino Imitators

06.1048　Florentine, 2nd quarter XV century

64.288　Florentine, 3rd quarter XV century

49.7.6　Master of the Castello Nativity

32.100.98　Giovanni di Francesco

15.106.1 Benozzo Gozzoli

15.106.2 Benozzo Gozzoli

15.106.3 Benozzo Gozzoli

15.106.4 Benozzo Gozzoli

1976.100.14 Benozzo Gozzoli

50.135.1 Cosimo Rosselli

32.100.84 Cosimo Rosselli

1975.1.73 Cosimo Rosselli

41.100.6 Master of San Miniato

48.78 Follower of Andrea del Castagno

14.40.647 Workshop of Andrea del Verrocchio

41.100.10 Jacopo del Sellaio

Italian / Florentine

61.235　Francesco Botticini

13.119.1　Domenico Ghirlandaio

13.119.2　Domenico Ghirlandaio

13.119.3　Domenico Ghirlandaio

80.3.674 Domenico Ghirlandaio

49.7.7 Domenico Ghirlandaio

32.100.71 Domenico Ghirlandaio

41.190.24 Follower of Domenico Ghirlandaio

14.40.642 Botticelli

49.7.4 Follower of Botticelli

1975.1.74 Botticelli

11.98 Botticelli

41.116.1 Follower of Botticelli

1975.1.61 Master of the Gothic Buildings

49.7.10 Filippino Lippi

12.168 Workshop of Filippino Lippi

43.86.5 Lorenzo di Credi

09.197 Lorenzo di Credi

50.135.3 Piero del Pollaiuolo

1975.1.77 Attributed to Amadeo da Pistoia

80.3.679 Florentine, last quarter XV century

14.40.641 Attributed to Raffaellino del Garbo

22.60.52 Piero di Cosimo

75.7.2,1 Piero di Cosimo

09.136.1 Biagio di Antonio

09.136.2 Workshop of Biagio di Antonio

32.100.68 Biagio di Antonio

32.100.69 Biagio di Antonio

1975.1.75 Florentine, late XV century

1975.1.76 Florentine, late XV century

14.40.635 Sebastiano Mainardi

32.100.67 Sebastiano Mainardi

1970.134.1 Francesco Granacci

1970.134.2 Francesco Granacci

06.171 Fra Bartolomeo

30.95.270 Mariotto Albertinelli

32.100.80 Ridolfo Ghirlandaio

30.83 Giuliano Bugiardini

1971.115.3a Giuliano Bugiardini

1971.115.3b Giuliano Bugiardini

Italian / Florentine

32.100.89 Andrea del Sarto

22.75 Andrea del Sarto

38.178 Bacchiacca

17.190.8 Tommaso Fiorentino

38

29.100.16 Bronzino

08.262 Workshop of Bronzino

55.14 Francesco Salviati

45.128.11 Francesco Salviati

30.95.236 Jacopino del Conte

1977.384.1 Jacopino del Conte

56.51 Paolo Zacchia

32.100.66 Florentine, middle XVI century

53.45.1 Florentine, middle XVI century

1976.100.15 Florentine, XVI century

1978.554.1 Francesco Curradi

80.3.245a Aurelio Lomi

69.283 Cesare Dandini

80.3.673 Volterrano

68.162 Florentine, 2nd quarter XVII century

ITALIAN PAINTINGS

SIENESE, XIV–XVI CENTURY

24.78 Segna di Buonaventura

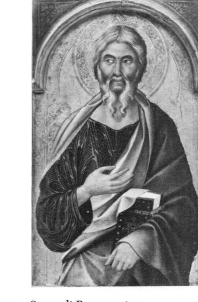

41.100.22 Segna di Buonaventura

1975.1.3 Segna di Buonaventura

1975.1.4 Segna di Buonaventura

65.181.2 Segna di Buonaventura

1975.1.6 Ugolino da Nerio

1975.1.5 Ugolino da Nerio

1975.1.7 Ugolino da Nerio

1975.1.1 Follower of Duccio

1975.1.2 Follower of Duccio

20.160 Goodhart Ducciesque Master

41.100.23 Simone Martini

43.98.9 Workshop of Simone Martini

43.98.10 Workshop of Simone Martini

43.98.11 Workshop of Simone Martini

43.98.12 Workshop of Simone Martini

Italian / Sienese

88.3.99 Lippo Memmi

64.189.2 Lippo Memmi

43.98.6 Lippo Memmi

1975.1.10 Follower of Lippo Memmi

49

18.117.1 Master of Monte Oliveto

41.190.31a–c Master of Monte Oliveto and a Sienese
Painter

41.190.26 Ambrogio Lorenzetti

13.212 Pietro Lorenzetti

1975.1.8 "Ugolino Lorenzetti"

1975.1.9 Sienese, active in Avignon, 1st half XIV century

61.200.1 Master of the Codex of Saint George

61.200.2 Master of the Codex of Saint George

41.190.531 Francesco di Vannuccio

32.100.100 Lippo Vanni

1975.1.12 Lippo Vanni

1975.1.13 Lippo Vanni

10.203.3 Sienese, dated 1343

1975.1.24 Sienese, XIV century

1975.1.14 Barna da Siena

1975.1.15 Barna da Siena

25.120.288 Bartolo di Fredi

1975.1.16 Bartolo di Fredi

41.100.14 Bartolo di Fredi

1975.1.11 Andrea Vanni

41.100.34 Luca di Tommè

25.79 Italian, Style of XIV century, XX century

1975.1.25 Sienese, XIV century

12.6 Andrea di Bartolo

55

41.190.13 Paolo di Giovanni Fei

1975.1.23 Paolo di Giovanni Fei

1975.1.22a Paolo di Giovanni Fei

1975.1.22b Paolo di Giovanni Fei

1975.1.21 Niccolò di Buonaccorso

1975.1.20 Niccolò di Buonaccorso

30.95.263, 265 Martino di Bartolommeo di Biagio

30.95.266, 264 Martino di Bartolommeo di Biagio

1975.1.17 Taddeo di Bartolo

1975.1.19 Taddeo di Bartolo

1975.1.18 Taddeo di Bartolo

1975.1.53 Benvenuto di Giovanni

1975.1.54 Benvenuto di Giovanni

43.98.1 Sassetta

41.100.20 Sassetta

1975.1.26 Sassetta

1975.1.27 Sassetta

1975.1.28 ab Sassetta

1975.1.29 Sassetta

1975.1.55–56 Pellegrino di Mariano

38.3.111 Giovanni di Paolo

41.100.4 Giovanni di Paolo

32.100.95 Giovanni di Paolo

1975.1.33 Giovanni di Paolo

1975.1.34　Giovanni di Paolo

1975.1.36　Giovanni di Paolo

06.1046　Giovanni di Paolo

1975.1.31　Giovanni di Paolo

1975.1.30 Giovanni di Paolo

41.190.16 Giovanni di Paolo

1975.1.38 Giovanni di Paolo

32.100.76 Giovanni di Paolo

1975.1.37 Giovanni di Paolo

1975.1.37 Giovanni di Paolo

32.100.83ab Giovanni di Paolo

32.100.83cd Giovanni di Paolo

975.1.35 Giovanni di Paolo

1975.1.32 Giovanni di Paolo

4.189.4 Sano di Pietro

41.100.19 Sano di Pietro

1975.1.39 Sano di Pietro

1975.1.40 Sano di Pietro

1975.1.41 Sano di Pietro

1975.1.42 Sano di Pietro

1975.1.43 Sano di Pietro

1975.1.51 Sano di Pietro

58.189.2 Sano di Pietro

58.189.1 Sano di Pietro

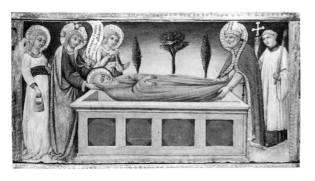

65.181.7 Sano di Pietro

1975.1.44 Sano di Pietro

1975.1.50 Sano di Pietro

1975.1.46 Sano di Pietro

1975.1.45 Sano di Pietro

1975.1.47 Sano di Pietro

1975.1.48 Sano di Pietro

1975.1.49 Sano di Pietro

20.182 Francesco di Giorgio

41.100.2 Francesco di Giorgio

11.126.2 Guidoccio di Giovanni Cozzarelli

14.44 Sienese, 3rd quarter XV century

41.100.37 Priamo della Quercia

41.100.35 Priamo della Quercia

41.100.36 Priamo della Quercia

41.190.22 Pietro di Domenico

61.43 Neroccio de' Landi

1975.1.57 Neroccio de' Landi

41.100.18 Neroccio de' Landi and Workshop

07.24.24 Copy after Neroccio de' Landi

07.241 Corrado Scapecchi

65.234 Matteo di Giovanni

1975.1.52 Matteo di Giovanni

41.100.17 Workshop of Matteo di Giovanni

73

41.190.29 Workshop of Matteo di Giovanni

88.3.100 Sienese, late XV century

41.100.38 Bernardino Fungai

26.109 Bernardino Fungai

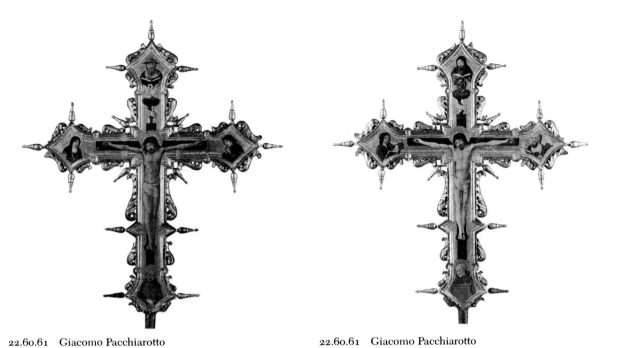

22.60.61 Giacomo Pacchiarotto

22.60.61 Giacomo Pacchiarotto

08.133 Sienese?, early XVI century

ITALIAN
PAINTINGS

CENTRAL AND SOUTH ITALIAN
LATE XIII–XVIII CENTURY

1975.1.104 Master of Saint Francis

1975.1.99 Marchigian, active about 1300

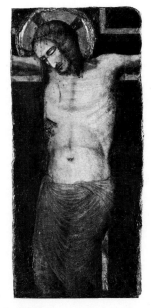

39.42 Pietro da Rimini

1975.1.103 Master of the Life of Saint John the Baptist

1975.1.105 Allegretto di Nuzio

1975.1.106 Allegretto di Nuzio

07.120.1 South Italian, early XV century

09.103 Riminese, middle XIV century

1975.1.102 Roberto d'Odorisio

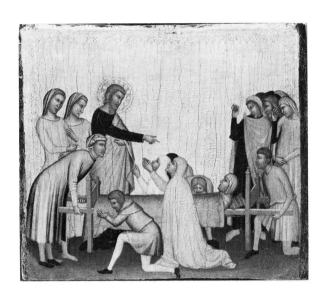

69.280.1 Francescuccio Ghissi

69.280.2 Francescuccio Ghissi

69.280.3 Francescuccio Ghissi

07.201 Pietro di Domenico da Montepulciano

30.95.262 Gentile da Fabriano

58.87.1 Bartolomeo di Tommaso

58.87.2 Bartolomeo di Tommaso

1975.1.100 Marchigian, middle XV century

1975.1.101 Marchigian, middle XV century

1975.1.108 Giovanni Boccati

1975.1.107 Niccolò di Liberatore da Foligno

11.65 Perugino

06.1214 Antoniazzo Romano

41.190.9 Antoniazzo Romano

30.95.290 Workshop of Antoniazzo Romano

35.121 Master of the Barberini Panels

1973.319 Saturnino de'Gatti

49.7.13 Luca Signorelli

29.164 Luca Signorelli and Workshop

32.100.74 Antonio del Massaro da Viterbo

14.114.1–4 Pinturicchio and Workshop

14.114.5 Pinturicchio and Workshop

14.114.6 Pinturicchio and Workshop

14.114.7 Pinturicchio and Workshop

14.114.8 Pinturicchio and Workshop

14.114.9 Pinturicchio and Workshop

14.114.10 Pinturicchio and Workshop

14.114.11 Pinturicchio and Workshop

14.114.12 Pinturicchio and Workshop

14.114.17 Pinturicchio and Workshop

14.114.18 Pinturicchio and Workshop

14.114.13 Pinturicchio and Workshop

14.114.14 Pinturicchio and Workshop

14.114.15 Pinturicchio and Workshop

14.114.16 Pinturicchio and Workshop

14.114.19 Pinturicchio and Workshop

14.114.20 Pinturicchio and Workshop

14.114.21 Pinturicchio and Workshop

14.114.22 Pinturicchio and Workshop

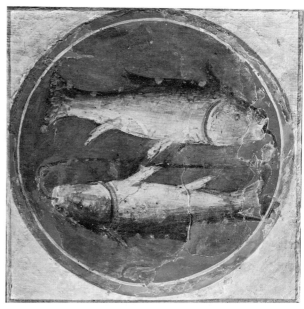

48.17.8 Baldassare Peruzzi

48.17.2 Baldassare Peruzzi

48.17.4 Baldassare Peruzzi

48.17.6 Baldassare Peruzzi

48.17.3 Baldassare Peruzzi

48.17.7 Baldassare Peruzzi

48.17.10 Baldassare Peruzzi

48.17.5 Baldassare Peruzzi

48.17.9 Baldassare Peruzzi

48.17.11 Baldassare Peruzzi

48.17.1 Baldassare Peruzzi

48.17.12 Baldassare Peruzzi

48.17.15 Baldassare Peruzzi

48.17.16 Baldassare Peruzzi

48.17.17 Baldassare Peruzzi

48.17.18 Baldassare Peruzzi

48.17.19 Baldassare Peruzzi

48.17.20 Baldassare Peruzzi

48.17.21 Baldassare Peruzzi

48.17.22 Baldassare Peruzzi

Central and South Italian

48.17.13 Baldassare Peruzzi

48.17.14 Baldassare Peruzzi

21.134.6 Andrea da Salerno

80.3.682–683 Attributed to Giovanni da Udine

16.30a Raphael

16.30b Raphael

2.130.1 Raphael

49.7.12 Copy after Raphael

14.25.1885 Central Italian?, 2nd half XVI century

28.181 Giuseppe Cesari

52.81 Caravaggio

59.40 Massimo Stanzione

30.31 Domenico Fetti

69.281 Artemisia Gentileschi

93.29 Michelangelo Cerquozzi

54.166 Giovanni Francesco Romanelli

1978.402 Mattia Preti

21.105 Salvator Rosa

34.137 Salvator Rosa

65.118 Salvator Rosa

43.23 Bernardo Cavallino

91.28 Workshop of Carlo Maratti

1973.311.2 Luca Giordano

61.50 Luca Giordano

07.66 Francesco Solimena

67.102 Francesco Solimena

71.172 Luca Forte

71.17 Giuseppe Recco

29.158.750 Neapolitan, 2nd quarter XVII century

1974.108 Pietro Bianchi

71.118 Giovanni Paolo Spadino

03.37.1 Pompeo Girolamo Batoni

Central and South Italian

89.4.1231 Roman?, XVII century or later

45.41 Roman?, late XVII/early XVIII century

86.20 Roman?, 3rd quarter XVII century

86.20 Roman?, 3rd quarter XVII century

37.160.16 Carlo Bonaria

71.31 Giovanni Paolo Pannini

52.63.1 Giovanni Paolo Pannini

52.63.2 Giovanni Paolo Pannini

07.225.293 Corrado Giaquinto

07.225.270 Workshop of Corrado Giaquinto

68.182 Gaspare Traversi

1976.100.19 Gaspare Traversi

ITALIAN PAINTINGS

VENETIAN, MIDDLE XIV–XVIII CENTURY

1971.115.5 Paolo Veneziano

1975.1.78 Lorenzo Veneziano

1975.1.79 Venetian, middle XIV century

1975.1.80 Venetian, middle XIV century

109

32.100.87 Master of Helsinus

23.64 Niccolò di Pietro

06.180 Michele Giambono

59.187 Jacopo Bellini

32.100.93 Venetian, 2nd quarter XV century

08.40 Venetian, 3rd quarter XV century

37.163.4 Antonio Vivarini

65.181.6 Workshop of Antonio Vivarini

1975.1.82 Bartolomeo Vivarini

30.95.277 Bartolomeo Vivarini

50.229.1 Bartolomeo Vivarini

65.181.1 Bartolomeo Vivarini

05.41.2 Carlo Crivelli

05.41.1 Carlo Crivelli

1975.1.84 Carlo Crivelli

13.178 Carlo Crivelli

49.7.5 Carlo Crivelli

1975.1.83 Carlo Crivelli

14.40.645 Antonello da Messina

32.100.82 Antonello da Messina

30.95.256 Giovanni Bellini

1975.1.81 Giovanni Bellini

08.183.1 Giovanni Bellini

49.7.2 Workshop of Giovanni Bellini

68.192 Workshop of Giovanni Bellini

17.190.9 Workshop of Giovanni Bellini

49.7.1 Giovanni Bellini and Workshop

41.100.32 Vittore Crivelli

1975.1.86 Jacometto Veneziano

1975.1.85 Jacometto Veneziano

49.7.3 Jacometto Veneziano

30.95.249 Antonello de Saliba

41.190.11 Giovanni Battista Cima

07.149 Giovanni Battista Cima

11.118 Vittore Carpaccio

65.117 Lorenzo Lotto

00.18.2 Sebastiano del Piombo

49.7.15 Titian

14.40.640 Titian

32.100.85 Titian

14.40.650 Titian

36.29 Titian

49.7.16 Titian

57.31 Style of Titian

27.56 Copy after Titian

1973.155.5 Domenico Mancini

30.95.258 Catena

69.123 Catena

Italian / Venetian

32.100.78 Bonifazio Veronese

1973.311.1 Paris Bordon

06.1324 Venetian, 2nd quarter XVI century

29.158.751 Venetian, middle XVI century

41.100.12 Tintoretto

58.49 Tintoretto

13.75 Tintoretto

39.55 Tintoretto

10.206 Tintoretto

49.7.14 Lambert Sustris

1973.116 Andrea Schiavone

89.4.2742 Girolamo Forni

46.31 Paolo Veronese

10.189 Paolo Veronese

29.100.105 Paolo Veronese

29.100.104 Francesco Montemezzano

125

14.25.1871 Venetian, late XVI century

29.158.754 Venetian, late XVI century

07.150 Venetian, late XVII century

1971.93 Carlo Saraceni

62.257 Jacopo Palma the Younger

57.170 Jacopo Palma the Younger

67.187.90 Giovanni Battista Piazzetta

06.1335.1b Gasparo Diziani

1975.1.87 Luca Carlevaris

1975.1.88 Luca Carlevaris

1975.1.89 Luca Carlevaris

1975.1.90 Luca Carlevaris

1970.212.2 Antonio Joli

65.183.1 Giovanni Battista Tiepolo

65.183.2 Giovanni Battista Tiepolo

65.183.3 Giovanni Battista Tiepolo

23.128 Giovanni Battista Tiepolo

71.121 Giovanni Battista Tiepolo

1977.1.3 Giovanni Battista Tiepolo

37.165.2 Giovanni Battista Tiepolo

37.165.1 Giovanni Battista Tiepolo

37.165.3 Giovanni Battista Tiepolo

37.165.4 Giovanni Battista Tiepolo

43.85.12 Workshop of Giovanni Battista Tiepolo

131

43.85.13 Workshop of Giovanni Battista Tiepolo

43.85.14 Workshop of Giovanni Battista Tiepolo

43.85.15 Workshop of Giovanni Battista Tiepolo

43.85.16 Workshop of Giovanni Battista Tiepolo

43.85.17 Workshop of Giovanni Battista Tiepolo

43.85.18 Workshop of Giovanni Battista Tiepolo

43.85.19 Workshop of Giovanni Battista Tiepolo

43.85.20 Workshop of Giovanni Battista Tiepolo

43.85.21 Workshop of Giovanni Battista Tiepolo

43.85.22 Workshop of Giovanni Battista Tiepolo

43.85.23 Workshop of Giovanni Battista Tiepolo

43.85.24 Workshop of Giovanni Battista Tiepolo

10.207 Canaletto

59.38 Canaletto

59.189.1 Francesco Zuccarelli

1975.1.91 Francesco Zuccarelli

135

Italian / Venetian

14.32.2 Pietro Longhi

14.32.1 Pietro Longhi

17.190.12 Pietro Longhi

36.16 Pietro Longhi

1.119 Francesco Guardi

71.120 Francesco Guardi

5.40.3 Francesco Guardi

35.40.4 Francesco Guardi

50.145.21 Francesco Guardi

41.80 Francesco Guardi

53.225.3 Francesco Guardi

53.225.4 Francesco Guardi

65.181.8 Francesco Guardi 1975.1.92 Francesco Guardi

1975.1.93 Francesco Guardi 1975.1.94 Francesco Guardi

1974.356.28 Francesco Guardi

32.75.5 Copy after Francesco Guardi

64.272.1 Attributed to Francesco Guardi

64.272.2 Attributed to Francesco Guardi

39.142 Bernardo Bellotto

29.70 Attributed to Maggiotto

50.78 Antonio Marinetti

35.26 Venetian, 2nd quarter XVIII century

1980.67 Giovanni Domenico Tiepolo

71.28 Giovanni Domenico Tiepolo

07.225.297 Giovanni Domenico Tiepolo

13.2 Giovanni Domenico Tiepolo

71.30 Jacopo Guarana

94.4.364 Giustino Menescardi

07.225.253 Francesco Casanova

15.118 Alessandro Longhi

ITALIAN PAINTINGS

NORTH ITALIAN
MIDDLE XIV – XVIII CENTURY

88.3.86 Guariento di Arpo

65.181.3 North Italian, 3rd quarter XIV century

43.98.7 Michelino Molinari da Besozzo

65.181.5 Antonio di Guido Alberti

37.163.2 Donato de'Bardi

37.163.3 Donato de'Bardi

37.163.1 Donato de'Bardi

1975.1.98 Cristoforo Morettis

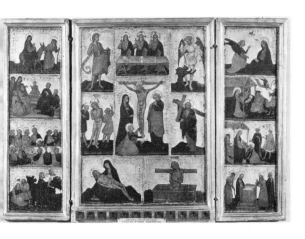

9.104 Veronese, 1st half XV century

32.100.96 Veronese, 1st half XV century

2.60.59 Bartolomeo degli Erri

23.140 Bartolomeo degli Erri

32.100.97 Andrea Mantegna

14.40.643 Andrea Mantegna

32.130.2 Andrea Mantegna

1975.1.109 Style of Andrea Mantegna

49.7.11 Style of Andrea Mantegna

14.40.649 Cosimo Tura

49.7.17 Cosimo Tura

30.95.259 Cosimo Tura

North Italian

30.95.293 Vincenzo Foppa

65.220.1 Francia

41.100.3 Francia

1975.1.97 Francia

4.40.638 Francia

32.100.94 Follower of Francia

9.102 Bartolomeo Montagna

14.40.606 Bartolomeo Montagna

43.98.8 Girolamo da Cremona

91.26.5 Giovanni Ambrogio de Predis

32.100.81 Andrea Solario

22.16.12 Andrea Solario

1975.1.95 Lorenzo Costa

1975.1.96 Lorenzo Costa

27.41 Michele da Verona

27.39.1 Bergognone

27.39.2 Bergognone

27.39.3 Bergognone

27.39.4 Bergognone

27.39.5 Bergognone

27.39.6 Bergognone

27.39.7 Bergognone

27.39.8 Bergognone

27.39.9 Bergognone

157

27.39.10 Bergognone

27.39.11 Bergognone

27.39.12 Bergognone

27.39.13 Bergognone

30.95.289 Boccaccio Boccaccino

30.95.292 Francesco Zaganelli

12.178.2 Bramantino

42.57.5 Giovanni Francesco Maineri

20.92 Girolamo dai Libri

15.56 Defendente Ferrari

17.190.23 Garofalo

17.190.24 Garofalo

58.182 Pseudo-Boccaccino

41.100.13 Bernardino of Genoa

12.57 Zenone Veronese

30.95.296 L'Ortolano

161

05.2.1 Lombard, 1st quarter XVI century

05.2.2 Lombard, 1st quarter XVI century

05.2.3 Lombard, 1st quarter XVI century

05.2.4 Lombard, 1st quarter XVI century

05.2.5 Lombard, 1st quarter XVI century

05.2.6 Lombard, 1st quarter XVI century

05.2.7 Lombard, 1st quarter XVI century

05.2.8 Lombard, 1st quarter XVI century

05.2.9 Lombard, 1st quarter XVI century

05.2.10 Lombard, 1st quarter XVI century

05.2.11 Lombard, 1st quarter XVI century

05.2.12 Lombard, 1st quarter XVI century

2.14 Giovanni Girolamo Savoldo

12.211 Correggio

6.83 Dosso Dossi

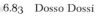

41.100.7 Calisto Piazza

30.95.246 Lombard, 1st quarter XVI century

11.53 Moretto da Brescia

28.79 Moretto da Brescia

12.61 Moretto da Brescia

23.188.1 North Italian, early XVI century

23.188.2 North Italian, early XVI century

23.188.3 North Italian, early XVI century

23.188.4 North Italian, early XVI century

North Italian

23.188.5 North Italian, early XVI century

23.188.6 North Italian, early XVI century

23.188.7 North Italian, early XVI century

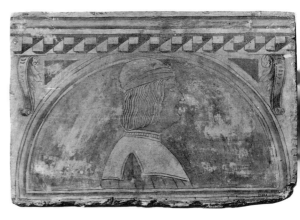

23.188.8 North Italian, early XVI century

3.188.9 North Italian, early XVI century

23.188.10 North Italian, early XVI century

3.188.11 North Italian, early XVI century

23.188.12 North Italian, early XVI century

169

23.188.13 North Italian, early XVI century

23.188.14 North Italian, early XVI century

14.25.1874 Ferrarese, 2nd quarter XVI century

91.26.2 Lombard, 2nd quarter XVI century

170

63.43.1 Bernardino Campi

13.177 Giovanni Battista Moroni

30.95.238 Giovanni Battista Moroni

30.95.255 Giovanni Battista Moroni

41.100.5 Bartolomeo Passerotti

32.100.88 North Italian, late XVI century

32.100.101 North Italian, late XVI century

62.122.141 Bolognese, late XVI century

1971.155 Annibale Carracci

1979.209 Giulio Cesare Procaccini

59.32 Guido Reni

1974.348 Guido Reni

27.93 Bernardo Strozzi

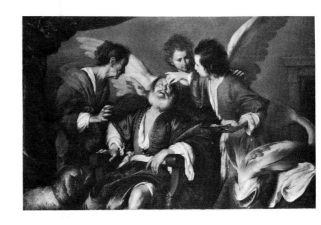

57.23 Bernardo Strozzi

1976.155.2 Domenichino

1973.311.3 Guercino

89.4.1224 North Italian?, XVII century or later

89.4.1224 North Italian?, XVII century or later

89.4.1222 Italian, XVII century or later

27.163 Alessandro Magnasco

1970.261 Bartolommeo Guidobono

1973.165 Francesco del Cairo

30.15 Giacomo Ceruti

54.61 Giacomo Ceruti

07.225.295 Carlo Carloni

08.237.2 Giovanni Raggi

ITALIAN
PAINTINGS

XIX CENTURY

47.71 Giovanni Boldini

59.78 Giovanni Boldini

08.136.12 Giovanni Boldini

87.15.81 Giovanni Boldini

08.136.13 Alberto Pasini

25.110.94 Alberto Pasini

92.1.62 Antonio Mancini

21.184 Giovanni Maldura

SPANISH PAINTINGS

including Portuguese and Peruvian

XII–XIX CENTURY

7.97.5 Spanish, XII century

61.219 Spanish, XII century

7.97.6 Spanish, XII century

59.196 Spanish, XII century

185

57.97.1 Spanish, XII century

57.97.2 Spanish, XII century

57.97.3 Spanish, XII century

57.97.4 Spanish, XII century

51.248 Spanish, XII century

50.180a–c Master of Pedret

55.120.3 Spanish, Style of XIII century, XX century

55.120.3 Spanish, Style of XIII century, XX century

187

Spanish

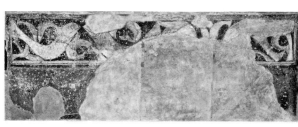

31.38.1a Castilian, early XIII century

31.38.1b Castilian, early XIII century

31.38.2a Castilian, early XIII century

31.38.2b Castilian, early XIII century

55.62a Spanish, last quarter XIII century

55.62b Spanish, last quarter XIII century

1977.94 Spanish, last quarter XIII century

57.49 Spanish, Style of XIII century, XX century

50.162 Catalan, late XIII/early XIV century

29.158.742 Catalan, late XIV century

25.120.257 Castilian, late XIV century

25.120.257 Castilian, late XIV century

57.50a Spanish, late XIV/early XV century

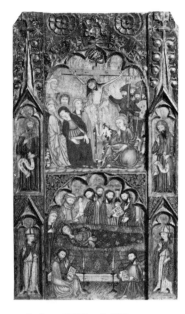

57.50b Spanish, late XIV/early XV century

57.50c Spanish, late XIV/early XV century

57.50d Spanish, late XIV/early XV century

Spanish

57.50e Spanish, late XIV/early XV century

57.50f Spanish, late XIV/early XV century

57.50g Spanish, late XIV/early XV century

32.100.123 Catalan, early XV century

192

06.1211.1–9 Catalan, early XV century

39.54 Valencian, early XV century

12.192 Valencian, 1st quarter XV century

76.10 Miguel Alcañiz

Spanish

52.35 Master of Riglos

32.100.126 Catalan, middle XV century

32.100.127 Catalan, middle XV century

32.100.128 Catalan, middle XV century

194

55.120.2 Master of Belmonte

32.100.105 Spanish, middle XV century

25.120.668–671, 673, 674, 927–929 Domingo Ram

38.141a–o Aragonese, late XV century

Spanish

29.158.744 Castilian, late XV century

88.3.82 Castilian, late XV century

10.12 Master of Bonnat

61.249 Spanish, XV century

196

44.63.1ab Spanish, XV century

44.63.1ab Spanish, XV century

44.63.1ab Spanish, XV century

44.63.1ab Spanish, XV century

Spanish

41.190.28a–d Aragonese, XV century

41.190.27a–e Castilian, XV century

58.145.1 Budapest Master

1976.100.24 Spanish, about 1500

198

29.158.745　Valencian, early XVI century

58.145.2　Frei Carlos

1978.416　El Greco

1975.1.145　El Greco

Spanish

61.101.8　El Greco

29.100.5　El Greco

41.190.17　El Greco

24.197.1　El Greco

1975.1.146 El Greco

05.42 El Greco

29.100.6 El Greco

56.48 El Greco

Spanish

25.110.21 Alonzo Sánchez Coello

1976.100.18 Alonzo Sánchez Coello

55.174 Attributed to Juan Pantoja de la Cruz

29.158.755 Spanish, late XVI century

202

45.128.15 Spanish, early XVII century

34.73 Jusepe Ribera

27.137 Francisco de Zurbarán

20.104 Francisco de Zurbarán

Spanish

1976.100.21 Francisco de Zurbarán

69.54 Francisco de Zurbarán

65.220.2 Francisco de Zurbarán

14.40.631 Velázquez

14.40.639 Velázquez

52.125 Velázquez

1975.1.147 Velázquez

1971.86 Velázquez

Spanish

49.7.43 Velázquez

89.15.18 Workshop of Velázquez

89.15.29 Workshop of Velázquez

49.7.42 Workshop of Velázquez

206

29.100.607 Castilian, XVII century

43.101 Juan Bautista Martínez del Mazo

27.219 Bartolomé Esteban Murillo

54.190 Bartolomé Esteban Murillo

Spanish

43.13 Bartolomé Esteban Murillo

1976.100.17 Bartolomé Esteban Murillo

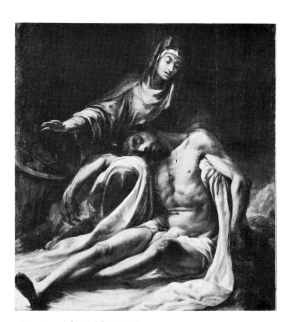

54.168 Juan de Valdés Leal

63.194.2 Spanish, XVII century

208

32.100.7 Andalusian, late XVII century

89.15.17 Andalusian, late XVII century

64.164.385 Peruvian, XVIII century

1975.1.148 Goya

Spanish

49.7.41 Goya

06.289 Goya

51.70 Goya

30.95.243 Goya

61.259 Goya

29.100.180 Goya

55.145.1 Goya

55.145.2 Goya

Spanish

29.100.10 Goya

30.95.242 Goya

22.181 Goya

29.100.12 Style of Goya

212

50.145.19 Copy after Goya

29.100.11 Copy after Goya

29.100.179 Style of Goya

83.11 Ignacio de Leon y Escosura

Spanish

89.22 Mariano Fortuny

08.136.14 Francisco Domingo y Marqués

15.30.71 Rico

81.1.666 Rico

214

87.15.57 Rico

25.110.81 Rico

04.29.1 Madrazo

87.15.131 Madrazo

Spanish

37.20.3 Madrazo

1975.1.233 Madrazo

87.15.39 José Villegas

87.4.7 Dionisio Baixeras y Verdaguer

216

30.22 Carlos Baca-Flor

39.119 Carlos Baca-Flor

09.71.2 Sorolla

22.119.1 Sorolla

Spanish

09.71.3 Sorolla

58.81 Sorolla

59.16.4 Ignacio Zuloaga

28.199 Ignacio Zuloaga

218

49.64 Ignacio Zuloaga

64.171 Ignacio Zuloaga

ICONS

Byzantine, Post-Byzantine, and Russian

XV–XIX CENTURY

31.67.8 Byzantine, XV century

29.158.746 Nicolaus Zafuri

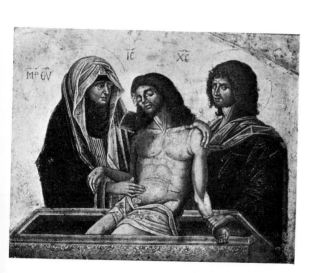

88.3.81 Post-Byzantine, Cretan, XVI century

33.79.19 Post-Byzantine, possibly Russian, XVII century

223

Icons

33.79.16 Post-Byzantine, Greek, XVII century

33.79.16 Post-Byzantine, Greek, XVII century

1972.145.30 Post-Byzantine, Greek, probably XVII century

31.67.9 Post-Byzantine, possibly XVII century

224

33.79.17 Ioannes Mokos

33.79.15 Emmanuel Tzanès

33.79.14 Emmanuel Tzanès

33.79.18 Emmanuel Tzanès

44.101 Russian, Novgorod, XV century

1972.145.27 Russian, XV/XVI century

1972.145.28 Russian, XV/XVI century

1972.145.24 Russian, XVI century

1972.145.33 Russian, XVI century

1972.145.13 Russian, possibly XVI century

1972.145.14 Russian, 2nd half XVI century

1972.145.19 Russian, late XVI/early XVII century

1972.145.23 Russian, possibly XVI century

1972.145.23 Russian, possibly XVI century

1975.87 Russian, XVI/XVII century

1975.87 Russian, XVI/XVII century

1972.145.26 Russian, XVII century

1972.145.29 Russian, XVII century

1972.145.16 Russian, possibly XVII century

1972.145.21 Russian, possibly XVII century

33.79.12 Russian, XVII/XVIII century

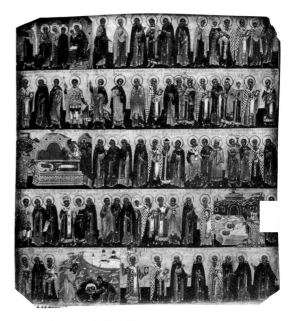

33.79.6 Russian, XVII/XVIII century

33.79.10 Russian, XVII/XVIII century

33.79.11 Russian, XVII/XVIII century

33.79.7 Russian, XVII/XVIII century

33.79.8 Russian, XVII/XVIII century

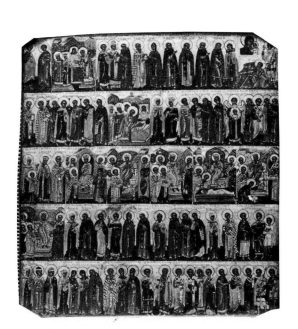

33.79.3 Russian, XVII/XVIII century

33.79.1 Russian, XVII/XVIII century

33.79.5 Russian, XVII/XVIII century

33.79.9 Russian, XVII/XVIII century

33.79.4 Russian, XVII/XVIII century

33.79.2 Russian, XVII/XVIII century

1972.145.17 Russian, late XVII/XVIII century

1972.145.31 Russian, XVIII century

1972.145.32 Russian, XVIII/XIX century

1972.145.35 Russian, XVIII/XIX century

Icons

68.160a Russian, about 1815

33.79.13 Russian, XIX century

89.2.108 Russian, XIX century

89.2.108 Russian, XIX century

234

54.58 Russo-Byzantine, XIX century

32.72 Russian, about 1890

1972.145.34 Russian, probably XIX century

1972.145.18 Russian, of uncertain date

1972.145.15 Russian, of uncertain date

1972.145.20 Russian, of uncertain date

1972.145.22 Russian, of uncertain date

1972.145.25 Russian, of uncertain date

1976.100.4 European, of uncertain date

RUSSIAN PAINTINGS

XIX CENTURY

1975.280.2 Ivan Constantinovich Aivazovski

1972.145.4 Alexei Kondratievich Savrasov

1975.280.6 Vassili Grigorievich Perov

1975.280.5 Constantin Igorovich Makowsky

1974.100 Arkhip Ivanovich Kuindji

1975.280.4 Ilya Efimovich Repin

1972.145.1 Ilya Efimovich Repin

1972.145.2 Ilya Efimovich Repin

1972.145.5 Vassili Dmitrivich Polenov

1972.145.3 Vladimir Igorovich Makovsky

29.63 Abram Yefimovich Arkhipov

1972.145.6 Mikhail Vasilievich Nesterov

BRITISH PAINTINGS

XVI-XIX CENTURY

91.26.3 British, dated 1539

20.151.6 British, dated 1572

51.194.2 British, dated 1588

11.149.1 British, XVI century

17.190.2 British, Style of XVI century, probably XX
 century

51.194.1 Marcus Gheeraerts the Younger

44.27 Robert Peake the Elder

06.1289 Daniel Mijtens

25.110.57 William Dobson

39.65.3 Sir Peter Lely

39.65.6 Sir Peter Lely

06.1198 Sir Peter Lely

British

39.65.9 Workshop of Sir Peter Lely

08.237.1 Robert Streater

39.65.8 Godfrey Kneller

96.30.6 Godfrey Kneller

250

56.224.1 Michael Dahl

39.65.7 Willem Wissing

60.94.2 Peter Monamy

32.53.2 John Wootton

20.40　Bartholomew Dandridge

56.190　Enoch Seeman the Younger

36.111　William Hogarth

91.26.1　George Knapton

05.32.3 Richard Wilson

15.30.42 Workshop of Richard Wilson

44.56 Samuel Scott

46.60 British, middle XVIII century

56.54.1 James Seymour

44.159 Charles Philips

39.65.5 Francis Cotes

69.104 Richard Cosway

42.152.1 Sir Joshua Reynolds

50.238.2 Sir Joshua Reynolds

48.181 Sir Joshua Reynolds

45.59.3 Sir Joshua Reynolds

British

10.58.3 Sir Joshua Reynolds

87.16 Sir Joshua Reynolds

20.155.3 Sir Joshua Reynolds

06.1241 Sir Joshua Reynolds

256

15.30.38 Sir Joshua Reynolds

54.192 Sir Joshua Reynolds

25.110.10 Sir Joshua Reynolds

05.32.1 Sir William Beechey

66.88.1 Thomas Gainsborough

60.71.7 Thomas Gainsborough

17.120.224 Thomas Gainsborough

50.145.16 Thomas Gainsborough

20.155.1 Thomas Gainsborough

45.59.1 Thomas Gainsborough

06.1279 Thomas Gainsborough

15.30.34 Copy after Thomas Gainsborough

89.15.8 Thomas Gainsborough

50.145.17 Thomas Gainsborough

45.59.5 George Romney

49.7.57 George Romney

58.102.2 George Romney

39.65.1 George Romney

50.169 George Romney

1975.1.235 George Romney

45.59.4 George Romney

15.30.36 George Romney

53.220 George Romney

15.30.37 George Romney

60.50a British, 3rd quarter XVIII century

1976.201.20 British, 2nd half XVIII century

49.7.55 Gainsborough Dupont

49.7.56 Gainsborough Dupont

46.13.5 Sir Henry Raeburn

96.30.5 Sir Henry Raeburn

65.181.13 Sir Henry Raeburn

1975.1.234 Sir Henry Raeburn

12.43.1 Sir Henry Raeburn

60.71.13 Sir Henry Raeburn

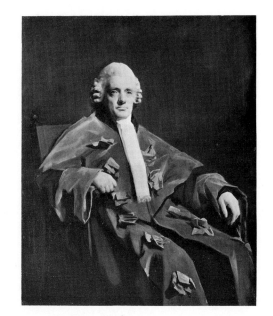

50.145.32 Sir Henry Raeburn

45.59.2 Sir Henry Raeburn

49.142 Sir Henry Raeburn

50.145.31 Sir Henry Raeburn

60.94.1 Sir Henry Raeburn

53.180 Sir Henry Raeburn

01.20 John Hoppner

15.30.41 John Hoppner

06.1242 John Hoppner

06.1242 John Hoppner

47.138　John Hoppner

53.59.3　John Hoppner

46.13.4　John Hoppner

46.13.3　John Hoppner

53.61.3 John Hoppner

53.113 John Hoppner

59.189.3 John Hoppner

65.203 John Hoppner

60.71.8 John Hoppner

60.71.9 John Hoppner

24.80.488 John Opie

43.132.4 George Chinnery

52.116 George Morland

25.110.20 George Morland

15.30.49 Francis Wheatley

51.30.1 William Blake

50.135.5 Sir Thomas Lawrence

12.43.2 Sir Thomas Lawrence

25.110.1 Sir Thomas Lawrence

55.89 Sir Thomas Lawrence

65.181.9 Sir Thomas Lawrence

59.91.2 Style of Sir Thomas Lawrence

59.91.1 Workshop of Sir Thomas Lawrence

95.27.2 George H. Harlow

273

95.22.6a James Green

95.22.6b James Green

99.30 Sir Martin Archer Shee

15.30.48 Sir Martin Archer Shee

89.15.14 John Crome

89.15.9 Joseph Mallord William Turner

99.31 Joseph Mallord William Turner

96.29 Joseph Mallord William Turner

British

06.1272 John Constable

50.145.8 John Constable

26.128 John Constable

15.30.50 Attributed to John Constable

276

1973.331.1 British, 1st quarter XIX century

1973.331.2 British, 1st quarter XIX century

05.31 William Etty

59.131 William Etty

British

15.30.52 Sir David Wilkie

96.25 Charles Robert Leslie

65.258.2 David Cox

15.30.56 Patrick Nasmyth

278

06.1300 George Vincent

1974.159 Frederick Richard Lee

97.41.1 James Stark

15.30.53 James Stark

97.41.3 Frederick Waters Watts

61.233 Edward Lear

45.146.1 Richard Parkes Bonington

45.146.2 Richard Parkes Bonington

1974.289.2 John Brett

10.58.2 British, XIX century

05.39.1 George Frederick Watts

04.29.4 John Thomas Peele

British

87.15.79 Frederick, Lord Leighton

96.28 Frederick, Lord Leighton

06.1328 Sir John Everett Millais

09.1.1 Philip Wilson Steer

282

47.26 Sir Edward Coley Burne-Jones

26.54 Sir Edward Coley Burne-Jones

22.177.4, 3 Style of Sir Edward Coley Burne-Jones

22.177.1–2 Style of Sir Edward Coley Burne-Jones

British

92.10.42 Robert Dudley

92.10.43 Robert Dudley

92.10.44 Robert Dudley

92.10.45 Robert Dudley

92.10.46 Robert Dudley

92.10.47 Robert Dudley

1979.135.15 Sir William Nicholson

1979.135.17 Walter Sickert

British

59.132 Roger Eliot Fry

09.179 Sir William Rothenstein

54.68 Frank Owen Salisbury

GERMAN PAINTINGS

including Austrian, Czechoslovakian, Danish, Hungarian, and Swedish

XV-XIX CENTURY

German

43.161 Master of the Berswordt Altar

1975.1.133 Bavarian, about 1450

32.100.38 Rhenish, about 1450

32.100.39 Rhenish, about 1450

German

53.21 Master of the Burg Weiler Altar

53.21 Master of the Burg Weiler Altar

64.215 Friedrich Walther

29.158.743 Rhenish, about 1480

290

26.52a Master of the Holy Kinship

26.52b Master of the Holy Kinship

44.147.1 Tyrolese, last quarter XV century

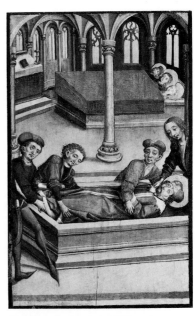

44.147.2 Tyrolese, last quarter XV century

71.33a Swiss, last quarter XV century

71.33b Swiss, last quarter XV century

71.40a Swiss, last quarter XV century

71.40b Swiss, last quarter XV century

1975.1.134　Westphalian, XV century

12.115　Ulrich Apt the Elder

71.34　Bernhard Strigel

23.255　Upper Rhenish, last quarter XV century

German

32.100.64 Dürer

14.40.633 Dürer

17.190.5 Attributed to Dürer

49.7.27 Style of Dürer

29.100.24 Lucas Cranach the Elder

29.100.24 Lucas Cranach the Elder

57.22 Lucas Cranach the Elder

1976.201.11 Lucas Cranach the Elder

295

28.221 Lucas Cranach the Elder

1975.1.135 Lucas Cranach the Elder

11.15 Lucas Cranach the Elder

08.19 Lucas Cranach the Elder

1975.1.136 Lucas Cranach the Elder

60.71.27 Attributed to Lucas Cranach the Elder

55.220.2 Workshop of Lucas Cranach the Elder

32.100.61 Workshop of Lucas Cranach the Elder

46.179.1 Workshop of Lucas Cranach the Elder

46.179.2 Workshop of Lucas Cranach the Elder

71.128 Workshop of Lucas Cranach the Elder

32.100.116 Swiss, 1st quarter XVI century

1975.1.137 Hans Maler

32.100.33 Hans Maler

14.40.630 Hans Maler

32.100.99 Augsburg, about 1525

17.190.21 Hans von Kulmbach

17.190.21 Hans von Kulmbach

21.84 Hans von Kulmbach

12.194 Barthel Beham

12.103 Ulm, 1st quarter XVI century

12.103 Ulm, 1st quarter XVI century

62.267.1 Barthel Bruyn the Elder

62.267.2 Barthel Bruyn the Elder

89.15.20 Attributed to Jörg Breu the Younger

32.100.50 Barthel Bruyn the Younger

07.245.1 Copy after a German Painter, middle XVI
century, XIX century

07.245.2 Copy after a German Painter, middle XVI
century, XIX century

50.145.23 Hans Holbein the Elder

06.1038 Hans Holbein the Younger

1975.1.138 Hans Holbein the Younger

50.135.4 Hans Holbein the Younger

German

50.145.24 Hans Holbein the Younger

49.7.28 Hans Holbein the Younger

49.7.29 Hans Holbein the Younger

49.7.31 Hans Holbein the Younger

304

49.7.30 Workshop of Hans Holbein the Younger

20.155.4 Copy after Hans Holbein the Younger

14.40.637 Copy after Hans Holbein the Younger

14.40.646 Copy after Hans Holbein the Younger

90.3.5 Franconian, dated 1548

90.3.5 Franconian, dated 1548

17.190.13–15 Attributed to Ludger Tom Ring the Younger

306

12.75 Conrad Faber

21.152.1 Georg Flegel

89.15.28 Jürgen Ovens

1971.115.2 Bernhard Keil

German

68.190 Abraham Mignon

50.50 Marten van Mytens the Younger

1978.554.2 Georg Christoph Grooth

34.83.2 Johann Georg Lederer

308

85.9 Christian Wilhelm Ernst Dietrich

71.162 Christian Wilhelm Ernst Dietrich

71.142 Christian Wilhelm Ernst Dietrich

59.189.2 Angelica Kauffmann

German

39.184.18 Angelica Kauffmann

39.184.19 Angelica Kauffmann

25.110.188 Angelica Kauffmann

25.110.187 Angelica Kauffmann

22.174 Johann Nikolaus Grooth

48.141 Anton Raphael Mengs

89.4.2741 German, early XVIII century

1971.115.6 Johann Eleasar Zeizig Schenau

311

German

89.4.3516　Franz Casppar Hofer

67.187.193　Attributed to Jacob Grooth

67.187.192　German, XVIII/XIX century

87.15.110　Wilhelm von Kaulbach

89.8 August Friedrich Pecht

01.21 Franz Xaver Winterhalter

1978.403 Franz Xaver Winterhalter

67.187.119 Franz Xaver Winterhalter

German

89.20 Julius Schrader

87.15.65 Johann Georg Meyer

87.15.132 Arthur Georg von Ramberg

87.15.23 Andreas Achenbach

314

87.15.33 Carl Georg Anton Graeb

23.103.3 August Xaver Carl von Pettenkofen

87.2 Carl Theodor von Piloty

87.15.105 Oswald Achenbach

German

26.90 Arnold Böcklin

26.100 Attributed to Arnold Böcklin

87.15.127 Adolf Schreyer

94.24.2 Adolf Schreyer

87.15.99 Alfred Wahlberg

25.110.68 Ludwig Knaus

64.151 Anton Dieffenbach

46.104.1 H. Hamm

87.22.1 Ferdinand Schaus

11.52 Franz von Lenbach

25.110.46 Franz von Lenbach

39.65.4 Franz von Lenbach

87.15.133 Hans Makart

09.48 Hans Thoma

87.15.58 Gabriel Max

16.148.1 Wilhelm Leibl

319

German

08.136.11 Mihály de Munkácsy

90.30 Gyula Benczúr

25.110.40 Hermann Kaulbach

17.120.203 Karl Hermann Fritz von Uhde

320

16.16 Hugo von Habermann

16.148.2 Max Liebermann

16.148.3 Friedrich August von Kaulbach

16.15 Wilhelm Trübner

German

1975.280.9 Fritz Steinmetz-Norris

17.204 Anders Zorn

19.112 Anders Zorn

60.85 Anders Zorn

322

67.187.116 Félix Vallotton

67.187.114 Félix Vallotton

67.187.115 Félix Vallotton

67.187.117 Félix Vallotton

German

20.33 Alphonse Mucha

54.33 Prince Eugen of Sweden